Introduction

> *"A garden should be in a constant state of fluid change, expression, experiment, adventure, above all it should be an, inquisitive, loving, but self critical journey on the part of it's owner."*
>
> **H E Bates**

Gardens can be gloriously colourful, laid out in formal patterns, quiet and contemplative or wild and overgrown. Each of these descriptions could stimulate your memories, responses and emotions and set up particular thought processes which could take you along a pathway of discovery with suggestions for ways of developing new ideas.

Gardens are one of the most popular topics for painters and textile artists to ponder upon and interpret in various media. As many embroiderers are also knowledgeable and enthusiastic gardeners it can at times be difficult for them not to portray gardens in a predictable way. We can never emulate nature so it is often wiser to endeavour to capture the very essence, memory or feeling of any exciting or stimulating feature that first appealed to you. Some aspects could be isolated and emphasised and certain areas exaggerated while simplifying or understating others. It is not necessary to try and represent them precisely. Colours can be spectacular or pale and subtle, plant forms enlarged or simplified, scale and proportions contrived to suit you. Use the information gleaned but allow your imagination to blossom.

This book hopes to offer suggestions and ideas to possibly revise your thoughts about creating unique stitched pieces inspired by a much-loved subject. Sensuous, evocative, memorable, unusual, pretty and witty are all words that we have considered when compiling this book. We hope that you will enjoy it and better still be moved to stitch your own interpretations.

Cover Image:
Letter from my garden *(detail).*
This folding letter (approximately 22 cms x 30 cms) celebrates the textures and patterns in my spring garden from the Montana clematis at the top to the fiddle top ferns opening up by the garden pond. It has been worked on a cotton ground which was built up in layers of bonded fabric shapes. In places, coloured 'Bondaweb' has been ironed over areas to give depth and to merge them into the background. Coloured chiffon scarves have also been applied to blend the imagery. Further bonded shapes were added before working hand and machine stitching. When all embroidery was complete the whole piece was applied to hand made paper and backed with cotton before being stitched along the creases of the divisions to give the folded effect. (JL)

Inside front cover:
A cloth of flowers celebrating joyous colour.
The ground fabric was coloured with transfer paints. The flower shapes were cut out with a finely pointed soldering iron and partially bonded to the background. Machine stitching was added to apply the shapes and highlight and drift colour throughout. (JB)

View of Jean's garden

View of Jan's garden

First thoughts...
or pathways to design

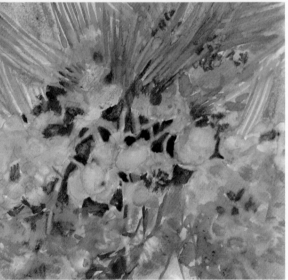

Above: *Sketches of a garden in Corfu coloured with aquarelle crayons. They inspired the formal arrangements shown opposite where certain aspects have been stylised and repeated to make a new design. (JB)*

Initially identify aspects of your garden that appeal to you. Colours can be subtle, vibrant, discordant and unexpected. For example, intriguing and surprising combinations can be found on stems of flowers and shrubs. They can be green, grey, maroon, red and violet and all the hues between. The sun setting low in the sky can shine through leaves highlighting such an array of greens, both vivid and startling. Bright sunlight also sets up wondrous shiny 'silver' flashes on the edges and surfaces of other foliage. Shimmery, smooth, silky, crumbly, encrusted, rough, grainy are words you may jot down to describe other surfaces. Remember how sensuous the feeling is when cupping a delicate or velvety petalled flower and inhaling its perfume or when running your fingers over and through soft blades of grass. Feeling the oxygen exuding from under a tree or being mesmerised by a soft breeze and the dappled leaf patterns of the shadows on the grass is always uplifting. Descriptive notes will help you capture these special moments and may be the first 'stepping stone' towards creating a design or adding interesting details to others.

Some of the following suggestions may be helpful in your initial thought processes:

• Select various images or shapes out of context and re-sketch them or interpret them in cut paper. Reassemble on a background in a seemingly spontaneous manner. Care should be taken when overlapping shapes so that these placements enhance and 'support' the background spaces which should also be pleasing and thoughtfully considered. Areas of similar tonal values and/or colour drifting through and linking all the elements will help to unify the design. (see cover)

• Once you have selected a section you can use your 'artists license' and emphasise one aspect while understating others. For instance, one variety of flowers could be featured and enhanced while the surrounding ones could be depicted with a hint of colour and a suggestive line. To illustrate this point iris leaves reflected in a pool could be partially abstracted and developed into an intriguing design of stripes in a wonderful array of greens. The choice is endless.

• Should you not want to (or not feel confident) to create an impressionistic or partially representative piece, formalising or stylising a design by setting shapes of flowers, leaves or other details within a pattern may be more suitable. Horizontal, vertical or diagonal stripes, diamond lattice or squares within squares could all be considered as possible frameworks to set in images, patterns, colours, textures, lettering or quotations etc. As with all design processes think about scale, choice of main and helping colours and contrasting 'busy' and 'quieter' areas.

Top: *This little bag front shows another pattern inspired by a 'primular' flower (see overleaf) set into a formal pattern. Snippets of fabric and thread were bonded onto the background cloth. All the embroidery was worked in Romanian couching some of which was layered, wrapped and beaded. (JB)*

These designs show a simple flower shape set in to varied arrangements.

• Another method of selecting a section out of context is to cut a paper or card frame of the desired shape. Place it on the drawing or photograph and move it around the surface of the picture pinpointing or highlighting the elements you like. Once you have selected the area you like draw the main shapes through onto some tracing paper. Take care to keep a focal point within the shape although not on an outside edge or absolutely centrally. This tracing can then be scaled up or down to the required size using a photocopier.

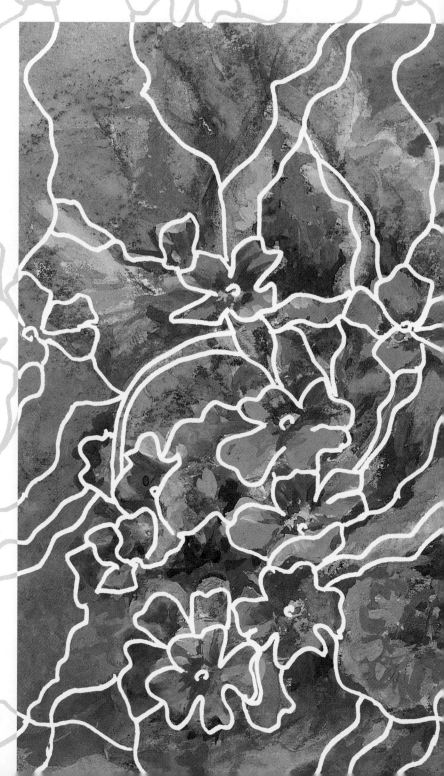

A painting of 'primula' plants worked in aquarelle crayons and gouache. A variety of paper frames were placed over the painting to select pleasing arrangements of colour and shape. The design opposite was made by repeating one of these selections to create a rhythmic all over pattern. (JB)

• Frameworks or structures found in the garden could also be used to help compose an interesting piece. Windows, archways, trellis, railings or pathway patterns would inspire a more symmetrical approach whereas selecting views through branches or foliage would offer a naturalistic setting. Remember to try varying viewpoints looking up, looking through, looking down!

• Designing an abstract or semi-abstract piece can be achieved by making a sketch, painting or a collage and cutting the images or photocopies up and re-assembling the pieces into several different arrangements. These could include squares, stripes, grids or haphazardly pieced strips woven in varying directions. The result could well capture the essence or mood of the subject without being too literal. These are well tried basic design exercises which are beyond fashionable traits and are always worth considering.

• Designing a cloth of repeating units and rhythmic elements can be created by selecting and simplifying certain characteristics. Tracing, photocopying or using computer techniques to repeat, arrange and link where necessary can create and maintain a pleasing result (see opposite page)

• You may wish to design in order to capture an idea, an image, an essence of a place, time or memory. These could reflect the passing of time or be a way of protesting or shocking the viewer into a response that was not necessarily comfortable. For example you may wish to express your feelings for or against the use of insecticides, organic produce, conserving wild flowers or encouraging butterflies or even feeling frustrated about the continuing battle with blanket weed invading your pond. In contrast your choice of inspiring words could include joy, happiness or celebration. Colours, surfaces, textures, directional marks, patterns or words could all contribute to helping you create a unique work.

• Themes or concepts may influence your thought processes. Warm, 'hot' colours may suggest a garden of love; golds and silvers to celebrate certain anniversaries, whereas historical personalities and events or fictional characters from books could easily set you on another train of thought.

It is challenging to depict an emotional response to a visual image. Ideally the technique should be there to support the idea, not the other way round.

Networks - *Inspired by the complex shapes in the intertwining stems of a clematis, this piece has been built up with several layers. On a ground of synthetic velvet a grid of open knitting using thick threads has been applied to form a base. A second layer of machine wrapped open work gauze added a contrast before applying machine wrapped cords. The sample was completed with freely worked buttonhole stitch and hand wrapping. (JL)*

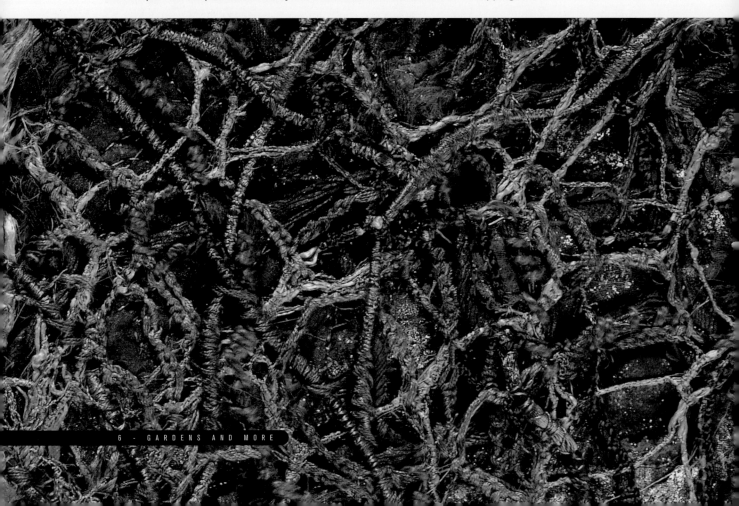

Growing Backgrounds

There are numerous ways to create an embroidered cloth using random, asymmetrical or symmetrical pattern arrangements. Sometimes predictable motifs decorate jackets, fronts of waistcoats, bags or cushions. They can look very attractive as long as the chosen pattern reflects or is sympathetic to the main shape of the item. A motif placed without regard to the background shape can look far too obvious and not at one with the main piece.

The general aim in this section is to suggest ways of creating an interesting background or cloth with an all over design. Having made a unique surface, the paper pattern of the chosen item can be placed on the cloth, cut out and made up as if you had purchased the material from a fabric store. The end result could look sumptuous, subtle and very individual. Flowers, leaves and stems could provide a super starting point. Initially walk around your garden, a park or a garden centre and fine tune your observations. Determine the main growth characteristics before worrying about the details. Make simple diagrams to denote the arrangements and directional growth of the stems. Are they curvy or entwining, pert and upward or elegantly arched and weeping. Some may meander along the ground through fences and trellis or contrast with other isolating sprigs or those

standing like sentinels. These are not meant to be botanical drawings so just relax and allow yourself to jot down the main lines as you see them.

In order to create repeating units of patterns:
Select and trace some of your diagrams several times placing them close to each other vertically, horizontally, diagonally or in half-drop arrangements. Take note of the background patterns as they form as you may wish to exaggerate these in your design. In some instances they could be developed to feature more than the initial diagrams. It may be necessary to contrive or slightly alter some lines in order to link and create pleasing rhythms. Photocopying one motif several times before cutting and pasting up to create the arrangements may be an alternative method of working. If you are a confident user of a computer, scanning in, repeating, flipping and inverting the image can give you endless design variations.

Simple diagrams showing the main lines of directional growth of a range of flowers. One of the patterns has been linked together to form an all over design. The fabric interpretation was coloured with transfer and silk paints with the design initially painted with masking fluid. (JB)

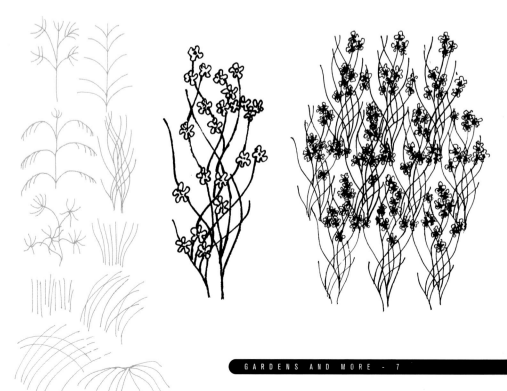

On finding a pattern that appeals to you, the following actions can be taken on choice of scale, colour, additional patterns and their placements. Vary the scale. A larger image may suit the project in mind. In some instances the same pattern worked in many sizes can give an effective result with a simple but unifying appearance. Make diagrams of flower shapes. Are the petals pointed, heart shaped etc? These flowers and leaves can be added to the linear image in a haphazard or symmetrical arrangement. The underpinning lines of the original design will help to keep the underlying unity. These extra images can be coloured or textured differently to add further interest and evolve a less predictable look. You may wish not to use the natural colours but prefer to develop the design in a range of reds or silvers and greys; whatever colour scheme is appropriate to your vision. Photocopying the design several times will enable you to try out several colourways. Take care to keep the tonal values compatible. Sudden very dark or light areas could spoil the unity of the cloth. Consider placing clearly defined forms contrasted with sensitive tracery of others if a subtle in and out of focus look is envisaged. Echoing finer lines also help link and integrate. If the design is to be developed as an appliqué, working the design in collage can be a helpful transitional action between the linear starting point and the building up of the fabric surface.

The example shown has been developed using several techniques including masking fluid resist and mono-printing with transfer paints, bonded appliqué, hand and machine

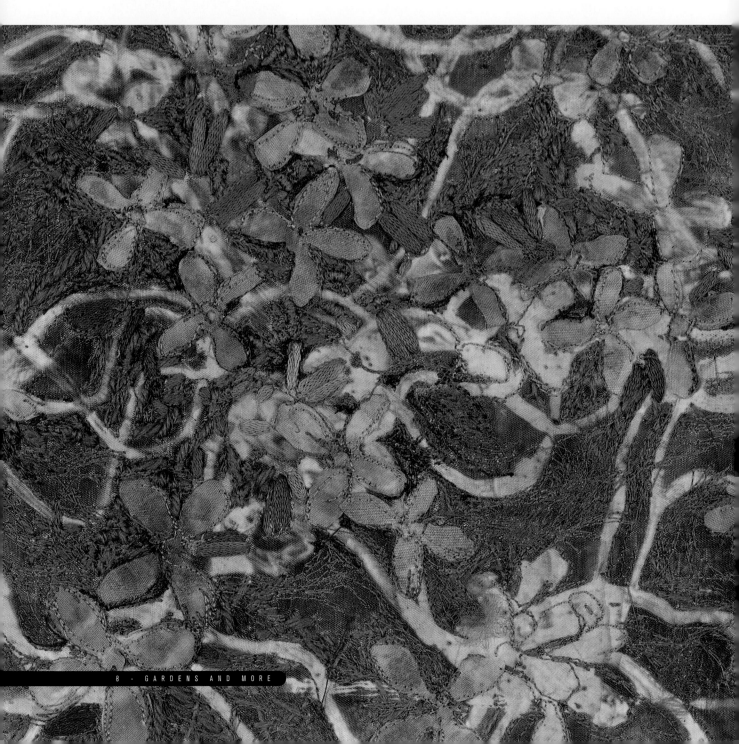

embroidery - all of which can be carried out in home studio situations. Those of you with access to screen printing facilities could produce lengths of fabrics where the motifs are repeated exactly, whereas the home based ones may not be so accurate but the quality and appearance will have an individual one-off characteristic.

The fabric interpretation was worked by bonding, hand and machine stitching flower shapes to a transfer printed ground cloth. (JB)

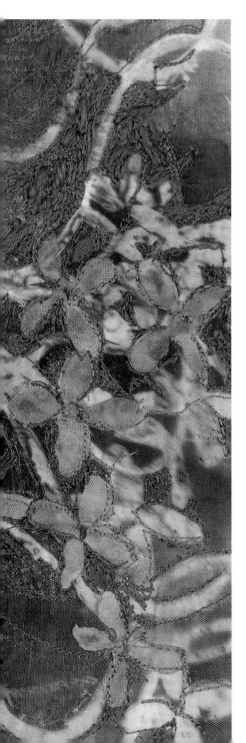

a.

b.

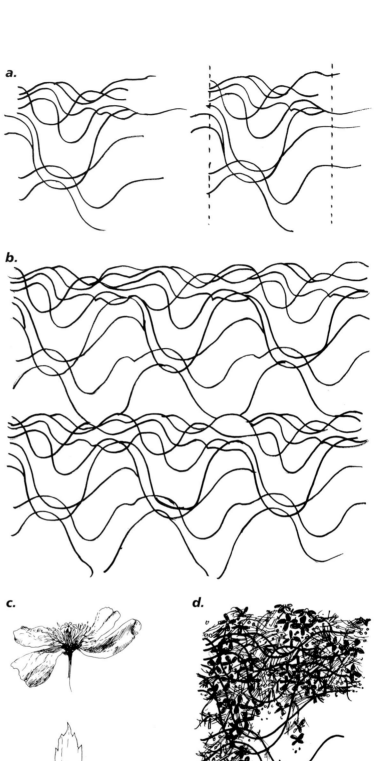

c.

d.

Montana clematis was the inspiration behind these illustrations.

a) The initial line diagram showing the basic stem structure. The second stage shows a cut off line in order to 'but' the units together easily to create an all over pattern.

b) Several units joined together

c) Sketches of the flower and leaf

d) Details added to the linear diagram.

Stitch a Flower or Leaf

Really looking and focusing your observations will improve your awareness as well as your drawing skills. Before attempting any mark making describe to yourself the shapes of certain flowers. Are they like stars, pendulous, rounded crosses, trumpets, tubular or deeply cupped? Do they cascade, scatter, stand erect or adorn tall spires? How would you describe the surface quality of the petals, like silk, tissue paper, velvet or firm and waxy? Follow these observations by noticing the leaves to include the shape, texture, markings, edge, method of joining the stem, the scale of the leaf to the flowers and of course the amazing range of greens or other colours. Stems offer surprising colours too and include reds, maroons, purples as well as shades of green. If you are wary of your sketching skills try drawing the shapes in the air with your hand. Other than being an odd action for others to observe you doing, your hand is such a blunt and bold 'instrument' that you will have to make simple movements. You will surprise yourself as these very actions will have initiated your first decision making it easier to follow on by making quick diagram sketches.

Many embroiderers love working French knots and they certainly are satisfying to sew. So many times flowers are depicted in this way but in actuality do not sport spot-like characteristics. Poppies, pansies, fuschia and others can be more often described as blips, blobs, blocks, splodges, splats, dots and dashes.

Try other stitches to capture these qualities. Vary the scale, encroach, overlap, layer and adorn. Remember to keep in mind the growth characteristics. Nature can never be equalled so experiment by enlarging, exaggerating, emphasising or understating in order to create a unique interpretation which is not attempting to copy but is endeavouring to capture the essence or qualities of the flowers which first caught your attention. Should you wish to stitch a garden with a more literal application be aware of and depict linking shadows and background shapes between the plants and shrubs. Think carefully about working isolated clumps in a variety of stitches which may 'compete' with one another. Some common thread of colour, texture or tone should run through the work to help unify all the parts. Fabric paint, applied fabrics, machine and handstitches could all be techniques to consider. A limited range of stitches but working them in varying sizes, threads and densities can give richer results.

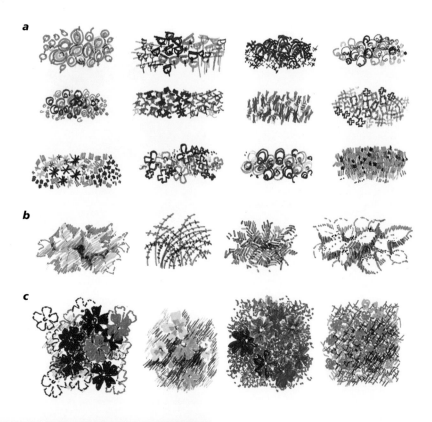

a

b

c

Above: A painting of a euphorbia plant, which displayed a beautiful mauve stem which made an attractive contrast to the new bright green leaves. (JB)

Left:
a) some suggestions for stitches to use to depict flowers. Notice the variations, size and placing. (from left to right)

- Detached chain
- Raised chain band
- Cross stitch
- Fused fabric beads
- French knots
- Sorbello stitch
- Short romanian couching
- Detached open chain
- Straight stitches
- Couching & seeding
- Detached double knot stitch
- Blocks of cretan stitch

b) straight stitches, bokhara couching and seeding shown depicting and linking the leaves.

c) Flowers linked and integrated to background by echoing the shape with running or couching stitches, straight, cross and seeding stitches.

The Supporting Cast

Flowers and shrubs are the first thoughts that come to mind when the subject of gardens arises but there are many other elements that are worth considering. Pathways, fences and sheds offer exciting alternatives. Pathways can be constructed in concrete blocks, bricks, crazy paving or interspersed with pebbles or gravel in a range of patterns. Those that are weathered, cracked, eroded or invaded by moss or ground-covering plants can be interesting to sketch and

may well suggest unusual combinations of colour, pattern and texture. Rain and frost give alternative effects. Wet surfaces often intensify the colours while frost can give a lacy, sparkling covering and transform a quite ordinary area into something very magical.
Wood, metal, wattle, wrought iron, plastic covered mesh are all materials used to construct fences and can influence the overall effect of any garden. They can be a marvellous foil to plants contrasting hard, smooth

or textured surfaces while the formal spacing of struts and bars offer a designer a number of alternative elements in which to base ideas. As well as being a supporting grid for a variety of plants they can provide an interesting framework for featuring views through and beyond. Misty, in and out of focus, impressionistic are all words that could influence you. Garden furniture, gazebos and other accessories can be too dominant to feature although sections of old sheds which sport peeling paint, the magical hues of rust, cobwebs, broken windows etc can come into their own. (see page 17) Taking some aspects out of context may be of more interest than some predictable floral interpretations.

Pathways of Thought - Mini Themes

Collections of snapshots, magazine cuttings, sketches and descriptive notes are all helpful information for the creative embroiderer. Notice boards, storyboards and flow charts can all aid the focus of your looking, develop ideas and possibly suggest some lateral thought processes to enable you to explore designs in an interesting and personal way.
An alternative method of focusing your observation is by looking at your garden through binoculars. You will be surprised by the many aspects that will be highlighted, isolated and enlarged and may give you ideas on how you could exaggerate and treat them in an individual way. There can be magical surprises such as rain drops suspending on the ends of a tracery of fine branches like a decorative Christmas tree or subtle rich colours within the shadows (see 'Apple Eaters').

We are all rather lazy and see our gardens with a familiar expectation. Highlighting with binoculars will refresh and review your observations. The flow charts shown on this page may suggest a number of starting points for a mini theme that you may find interesting. Many of the words listed could each in turn spawn another idea that could lead on to a fascinating body of work. The following pages illustrate some of these and other thought processes developed further with comprehensive notes to lead you along lateral creative paths.

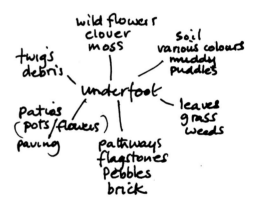

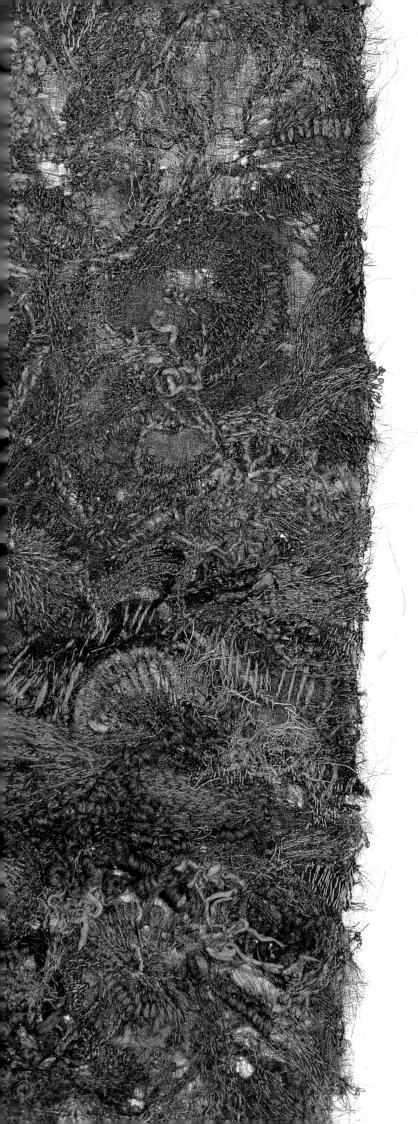

Above: *A sketch of rotting apples and decaying leaves which informed the panel opposite. Pencil and aquarelle crayons.*

The Apple Eaters - *Fieldfares among rotting apples under the old apple tree. Applied fabrics, hand and machine stitching (JB)*

Damage & Decay

The aim of the dedicated gardener is to nurture a colourful celebration of luxuriant patterns and textures. Dying plants and insect damage would be stamped out at source in a well-ordered regime. There is hope for those of us who are less than perfect in this respect as the colours and patterns of damage and decay can provide excellent opportunities for inspired colour schemes and atmospheric imagery. So instead of tweaking out dying leaves or dead heading everything in sight look carefully at the colours, which change from day to day and find a potential source of great beauty. Recording the changes and making notes with colouring media or torn strips of colour magazine will provide inspirational colour combinations for future use.

It is also possible to press the leaves or flowers but in the drying out process the vibrancy of the colours is dulled down and can be disappointing. Some plants, particularly those with succulent, fleshy leaves, will rot down over a period of time to provide delicate skeletal structures. When dredging a pond, the most wonderful, flexible, skeletal magnolia leaves emerged having been immersed in mud through the winter. Whilst there are well-documented ways of speeding up this process, finding them in the natural course of events is very satisfying.

Drifts of fallen petals on a path or floating on a pond could also spark an idea for a piece of work.

Slugs and snails are unwelcome in most gardens but even they have their redeeming points. When they break down the full range of countermeasures and get through to the Hostas the lace-like patterns have a fragile beauty which could inspire a range of gossamer surfaces to be worked by hand or machine embroidery.

Amazingly, slugs are quite colourful when viewed dispassionately. Iridescent bronzes and blues are reflected of their writhing forms. Discarded snail shells also display subtle patterns and colour schemes. Along with the destructive elements there are the wonderful flashes of vivid turquoise as a dragonfly flies past or butterflies flit in fragile shudders to add an ephemeral dash to the foliage.

Even a brief look around most gardens will reveal an interesting piece of rust or a rotting garden shed that offers excellent opportunities for design and so look carefully at your garden and try to find the beauty in the decay (see page 17).

Colour Photocopier

Drawing and painting are the best way of really observing the sources of inspiration and gaining a thorough knowledge of the way in which the plants grow and how the leaves and petals join onto the stems. Photographs can help to set the context and reinforce the drawing and a photocopier may offer some imaginative avenues for promoting ideas.

Decaying leaves will photocopy well and can be enlarged and reduced. The colour balance can be adjusted to gain a true colour or exaggerated colour depending on the desired effect. A colour photocopier can usually reproduce a 'negative colour' effect and this can be absolutely fascinating. Suddenly a familiar object takes on a startlingly different look that could inspire a fresh approach to designing from plant forms.

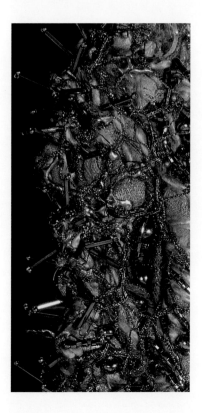

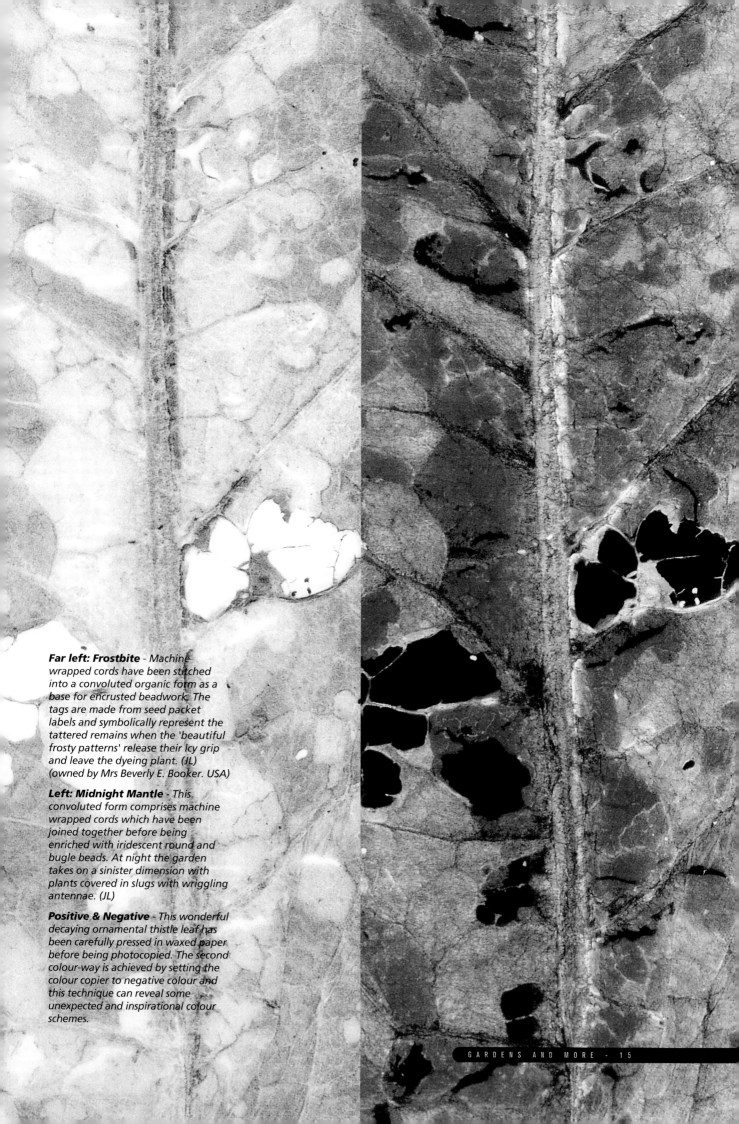

Far left: Frostbite - Machine wrapped cords have been stitched into a convoluted organic form as a base for encrusted beadwork. The tags are made from seed packet labels and symbolically represent the tattered remains when the 'beautiful frosty patterns' release their icy grip and leave the dyeing plant. (JL) (owned by Mrs Beverly E. Booker. USA)

Left: Midnight Mantle - This convoluted form comprises machine wrapped cords which have been joined together before being enriched with iridescent round and bugle beads. At night the garden takes on a sinister dimension with plants covered in slugs with wriggling antennae. (JL)

Positive & Negative - This wonderful decaying ornamental thistle leaf has been carefully pressed in waxed paper before being photocopied. The second colour-way is achieved by setting the colour copier to negative colour and this technique can reveal some unexpected and inspirational colour schemes.

UnderFoot

A garden is so full of opportunities for design that restricting the options will often be a profitable line to pursue. As an example 'underfoot' could be a good place to start.
Walking around a garden with bare feet and recording the contrasting sensations will highlight the soft, succulent texture of a moist lawn, or the hard gritty nature of a stone path. Fallen petals and leaves will lie in inspirational drifts which would be hard to contrive but work well in the natural setting. Nuts, fruits, berries and stones along with feathers and discarded snail shells could prove an excellent starting point for design. Patches of plants breaking through pathways, silvery snail trails, debris from a storm, a daisy lawn and moss covered flag stones are there to be drawn on for inspiration. Other peoples garden paths, exotic gardens, wild gardens and public gardens could also be developed in this way and once started it could be a theme for life and provide an alternative interpretation for the phrase 'up the garden path.'

Left: Footpath - Underfoot - *Some piled up dried grass cuttings were placed between two layers of painted 'Bondaweb' and baking parchment before being ironed to fuse them together. The piece was left to cool off for fifteen minutes before peeling away the parchment. Nylon chiffon scarves were ironed to back and front of the piece and the heat gun used to shrivel away the background into lace-like shapes. Having stabilised the grasses in this way it was applied to synthetic velvet before being enriched with hand stitching. (JL)*

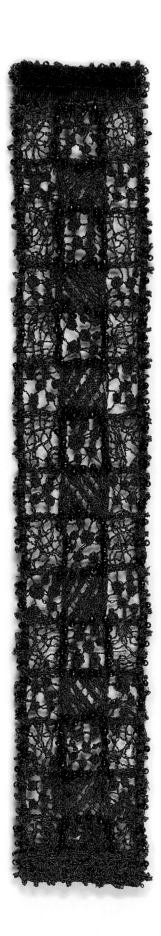

Left: A bracelet or decorative cuff worked in machine stitching on soluble fabric. Tiny beads and some hand stitching develop the surface further. The design was based on a wonderful, formally patterned pathway of varying stones and pebbles seen in a Chinese garden in Vancouver.(JB)

Above: Rusty Shed - The ground fabric was coloured with transfer paints and then enhanced with bonded layers. The foliage was achieved with the 'trapping' method described in the 'Underfoot' sample (page 16). Having worked bold hand stitches, machine stitching was used to blend the textures. (JL)

Right: 'Dig for Victory' - Pincushion. Inspired by the wartime thrifty use of space in gardens, this 'flight of fancy' has movable cabbages and lettuces pins on a patriotic theme. (JL)
(see page 22)

The Vegetable Patch

There are so many exotic vegetables around now that the potential for colour pattern and texture is immense.

Skin properties, seeds, cross sections, transverse sections, ripe and unripe flesh, and of course decay are the starting points for a huge array of ideas. Simple observations of even the most humble of vegetables will offer wonderful scope for stitched textiles.

The Savoy cabbage has a soft, rippled undulating quality and if at first the thought of drawing it is daunting take a leaf and explore the patterns of a small section, noticing the rhythms and cellular patterns. The vein structure has a logical and organic system which would be a good starting point for a structured cloth. The underside of the leaf has concave ripples and the upper side soft convex nodules. Write notes on the texture, the look and the feel. The more you draw, the more you will learn, and time spent learning about your source is never wasted.

Printing with vegetables will also offer many further ideas. These could be worked on paper using a variety of media or directly onto cloth using fabric paints. Transfer paints would be ideal for use with vegetable prints, which after being printed onto paper could be ironed off onto cloth in a variety of ways.

Cabbage drawing *-*
Sketchbook Page Cabbage leaf studies using watercolour, aquarelle pencils and wax crayon resist.(JL)

Hand Into Machine Stitch

The undulating surface of the cabbage suggested an integrated cloth using hand and machine stitching methods.

The deliberate use of bold hand stitch to be worked into later by machine is an underused technique and particularly useful for this organic source.

The 'nodules' were created by working knotted cable chain stitch into a linen ground using a thick silk thread. The veins were worked in bold couching When the hand stitching was complete machine stitching was worked carefully into the image to produce a blended cloth and this takes practise but is not difficult if the following guidelines are followed.

• Frame the fabric firmly and set the machine for free embroidery.

• Tonal values are most important if successful blending is required so select the colour of the machine thread carefully.

• If contrast is called for, machining with a complementary colour can offer impact with delicacy.

• Analyse the pattern or texture of the hand stitching and use machine rhythms that will enhance, not swamp, the image.

• When working round knobbly stitches slow the machine and stitch with care to avoid penetrating thick knotted areas. It is possible 'nibble' gradually into the stitches without covering them and blend in this way.

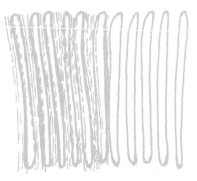

• When working on layers it may be possible to work without a frame or support the work with soluble fabric. There are times when the distortions created when working without a frame can be an asset.

• Before embarking on a substantial piece of work some simple exercises will help in developing sensitivity to this useful technique.

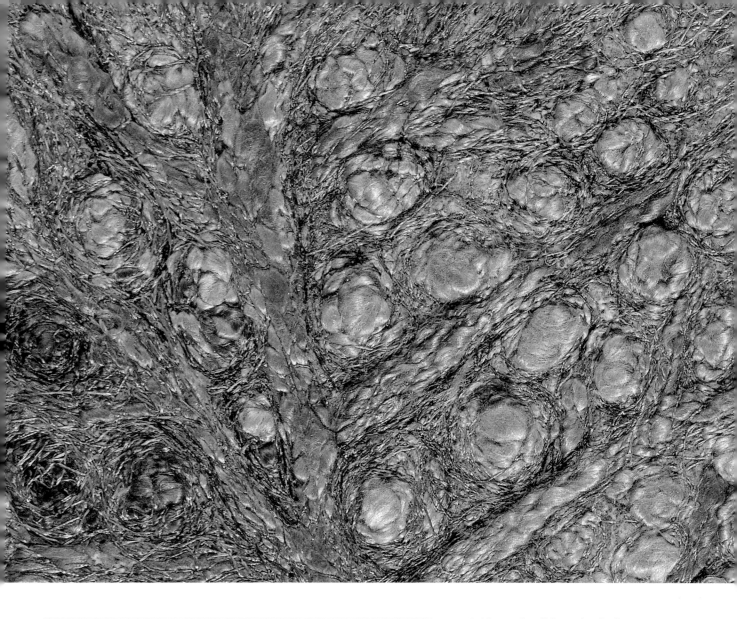

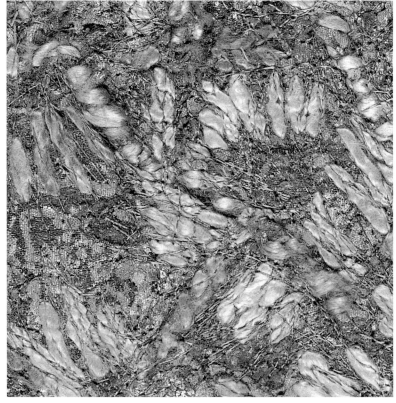

Cabbage detail (green) - The basis of this textured piece is a heavily worked background using hand couching for the leaves and knotted cable chain for the 'knobbly' textures. Machine stitching using sympathetically coloured threads were then worked carefully into the stitching to enhance but not overwhelm the stitches. (JL)

Cabbage (purple) - The background was first coloured with transfer paints before trapping fabric scraps with 'Bondaweb' and a chiffon scarf. The fabric was then manipulated into ridges before being overcast with hand stitching. Further hand stitching was then worked into with machine stitching to blend into an integrated cloth. (JL)

Far left: Cushion - Black discharge velvet formed the base of this richly stitched cushion. An all-over pattern using a stencil and coloured discharge paste gave a turquoise base for the stitching. Thick, bold threads were stitched using straight stitches and French knots were worked in a stylised floral pattern before machining which echoed to hand stitching for maximum impact and to avoid flattening the stitches. (JL)

Left: Transfer fabric paints printed onto synthetic velvet set up the background for bonded flower and leaf shapes. Hand and machine stitching developed an interesting although flattish surface which could be suitable for an all over cloth for a waistcoat, jacket or bag. (JB)

Above: Cascade of Flowers - An abundance of dark blue, purple and maroon pansies inspired this piece. The layers of petals were intriguing. Machine embroidery was worked on soluble fabric. (JB)

Flights of Fancy

The garden is just the beginning and ideas will emerge much faster than the ability to keep up with them. Here, the garden notebook will be really useful for recording information and noting down thoughts or ideas as they occur. Books on gardening are not only useful for the practical gardener but the designer might find the odd germ of an idea that could inspire a piece of work.

It was in just such a book of helpful advice that it was suggested that the dedicated gardener would need her garden gloves to enable her to preserve her hands whilst tackling even the thorniest bushes. Garden gloves could take many forms; what would they look like? True gardeners could be said to have 'green fingers'? People with 'green fingers' have great success in growing things; everything they touch blossoms. From such musings emerged the idea of garden gloves for the perfect gardener. Naturally the perfect gardener would also need to shade her eyes from the sun and keep the insects away from her face so a 'garden hat' might be needed to go with the gloves and so on...

Books also give us wonderful insights into the history of gardens that are the source of endless inspiration. The philosophies of gardeners such as Vita Sackville West and Mrs Delaney offer wonderful advice on colour and texture. The mere thought of the 'White Garden' created by Vita Sackville West could inspire a whole range of subtle yet richly textured imagery exploring this theme.

Mrs Delaney talked in terms of drifts of colour naturally merging into the wooded perimeters of her carefully constructed gardens. The colourful scrolling patterns of the Elizabethans contrast with the intensely worked Ayrshire embroidery but both celebrate a love of flowering forms.

The gardens of the 2nd World War were given over to vegetables as the country was encouraged to 'Dig for Victory.' This was also the time of 'make do and mend' and so the idea of a pincushion incorporating both of these ideas came into being. The background fabric of the pincushion is an old 1940's tray-cloth and it explores the idea that everywhere there was a space people planted vegetables and many of the cabbages and lettuces are on pins and so can be moved. (see page 17)

Sometimes all that is left of a once glorious plant is the sad little tag rather like a memorial. Having collected them for future reference and to avoid repeating the mistake they looked quite attractive as objects and so another idea was born, - textile garden tags. These ideas are a simple illustration of what happens when you allow your mind to wonder and take off on a garden 'flight of fancy.'

Tags - *Sometimes all that is left of the plant is a shrivelled stem and a colourful tag. These are worked in a range of techniques and using hand and machine stitching. Two of the tags have been printed by photocopying the seed packet onto transfer paper before ironing off onto the fabric and enriching with stitching. One tag features a trapped dried pansy flower under a chiffon layer with additional stitching to embellish. All tags have been mounted on felt before the lettering was worked with machine embroidery. (JL)*

The Ultimate Gardeners' Hat & Gloves - *The gloves have been hand knitted by Dorothy Sheldrake (Jean's mum) before being dyed green and overstitched with an irregular network of buttonhole stitch. To this structure has been added applied velvet flowers and assorted manipulated floral and organic shapes to achieve a 'full blown' overgrown look. Similarly 'overt' is the hat which has been worked on a crocheted shape covered in buttonhole stitch before being completely covered with an assortment of hand made and bought flowers and leaves. The hat was then 'dressed' with transfer painted net to complete. (JL)*

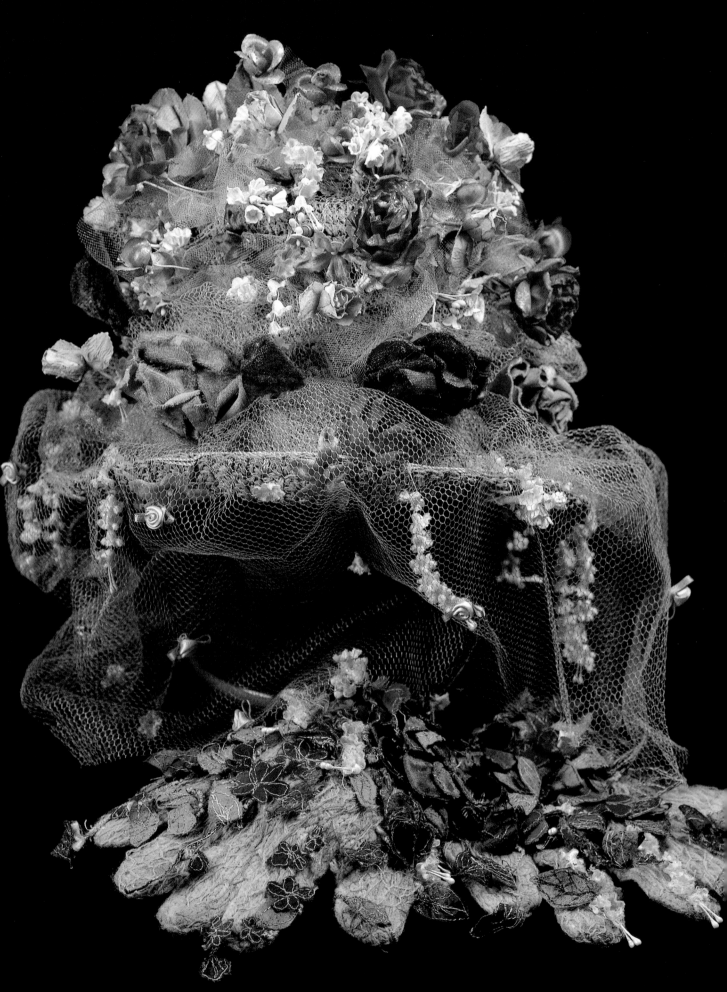

Conclusion

Draw and photograph views and close ups, all weathers, all seasons and all times of the day. Always accompany these actions with your own informative notes on colour schemes, textures, patterns, as well as descriptions of atmosphere, how you were feeling and the reason you were there.

A photograph will remind you of shape and scale but it is your personal notes that will add significant pointers to help you accentuate and exaggerate the particular features that first attracted you. Poems, prose and song could all be wonderfully inspiring starting points so always collect as much information as you can. This very personal information will help you develop and create original work.

Acknowledgements

Our heartfelt thanks go to our husbands for their continued support and to Victoria Udall for typing the text. We especially appreciate and thank Jason Horsburgh for designing the layout and Micheal Wicks for his super photographs.

Double Trouble Enterprises
PO Box 348, Maidenhead
Berkshire SL6 6XB UK
fax: +44(0) 1628 657699

Other books available are:
• Vanishing Act (JB)
• Voluptuous Velvet (JL)
• Bonding & Beyond
• Transfer to Transform
• Conversations with Constance
All by Jan Beaney - Jean Littlejohn. They have also written, 'A Guide to Creative Embroidery' & 'Stitch Magic' both published by Batsford Books

Left: This little bag was inspired by lace cap hydrangea. The designs were worked in machine embroidery on soluble cloth to create this delicate lace work. Separate flowers and beading were applied to add further interest. (JB)

Inside cover:
This sample was inspired by Wattle flowers sketched in Australia. The vivid lime yellow flowers and the elegant branches were sewn in variations of Romanian couching on a ground cloth bonded with chiffons and scrims to set up the initial tonal and colour placements. Some areas were machined to develop the dimensional surface (JB)

First published by Double Trouble Enterprises. ISBN No. 0-9531750-4-9

Distributors in North America Quilters' Resource Inc, PO Box 148850, Chicago, IL 60614. Phone 773 278 5695